MW01067823

KAMEHAMEHA III:
KAUIKEAOULI

Jean Iwata Cachola

Illustrated by
Robin Yoko Burningham

Kamehameha Schools Press
Honolulu
1995

KAMEHAMEHA SCHOOLS BERNICE PAUAHI BISHOP ESTATE

Copyright © 1995 by
Kamehameha Schools Bernice Pauahi Bishop Estate

Inquiries should be addressed to:
Kamehameha Schools Bernice Pauahi Bishop Estate
Media and Publications Department
1887 Makuakāne Street
Honolulu, Hawai'i 96817

The paper used in this publication meets the minimum requirements
of American National Standard for Information Sciences—
Permanence of Paper for Printed Library Materials, ANSI Z39.48-1984.

Printed in the United States of America

ISBN 0-87336-033-8

Cover photo courtesy of Bishop Museum

Dedicated to

the young people

of Hawai‘i

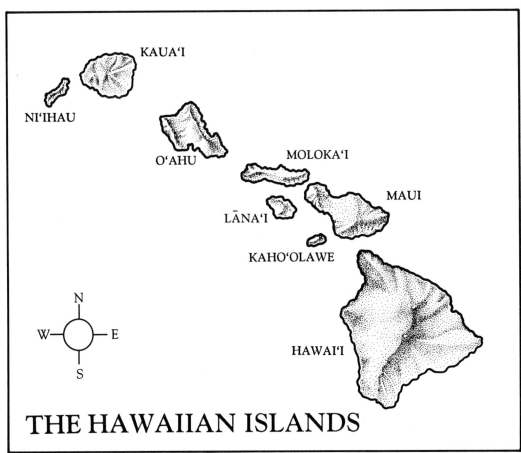

KAUA‘I

NI‘IHAU

O‘AHU

MOLOKA‘I

LĀNA‘I

MAUI

KAHO‘OLAWE

N

W—E

S

HAWAI‘I

THE HAWAIIAN ISLANDS

·R BURNINGHAM·

Table of Contents

Preface

This book is one of a series written for Kamehameha Schools Intermediate Reading Program (KSIRP) students. They are designed to increase students' reading skills and their knowledge of Hawaiian history and culture by focusing on topics such as the Hawaiian monarchy.

The books are written by KSIRP staff in an effort to provide young readers with culturally relevant materials in language arts and Hawaiian studies. The authors are pleased that the books have been well received by both educational and general audiences.

The books are being translated from their original English text into Hawaiian through the efforts of the staff of the Hawaiian Studies Institute (HSI).

Both KSIRP and HSI are Community Education Division programs of Kamehameha Schools Bernice Pauahi Bishop Estate. KSIRP is operated in collaboration with the State of Hawai'i Department of Education at several intermediate schools throughout the state.

Michael J. Chun, Ph.D.
President
Kamehameha Schools

Acknowledgments

*K*amehameha III: Kauikeaouli was completed with the support of family and colleagues and friends.

I first wish to express my warmest appreciation to my husband Fred and my daughter Lisa for their patience, understanding and encouragement.

Of the staff of Kamehameha Schools Bishop Estate, I am very grateful to *Julie Stewart Williams,* director of the Intermediate Reading Program, who edited the manuscript for grammatical accuracy, clarity of expression and reviewed the section on land ownership; *mahalo* to *Naomi Noelani Chun,* reading teacher with the Intermediate Reading Program, who ensured the proper use of Hawaiian and who also made significant contributions to the section on land ownership; deepest appreciation to *Russell Kawika Makanani,* teacher of Hawaiian History and Culture at the secondary schools, who volunteered many hours of his own time reviewing the manuscript for cultural and historical accuracy; and warmest gratitude to *Robin Yoko Burningham,* graphic designer with the Media and Publications Department, for her calmness and patience and whose beautiful illustrations greatly enhance the text.

J.I.C.

Kauikeaouli, Kamehameha III

Kauikeaouli

Mele Hānau

Hānau Kū, 'o Kū la auane'i ho'i kō luna.
'O wai la ho'i kō lalo nei, 'o wai la?

'O Hāloa, puka kānaka, laha nā ali'i.
Loa'a i luna nei 'o Ka-lani Mehameha,
'Ekāhi ka lani la, 'ekāhi o luna nei.
'O Ka-lani Kau-i-ka-'alaneo 'elua o luna nei.
Pili lāua, ua mau paha, 'oia paha?
'O Ka-lani-nui-kua-liholiho 'akāhi,
I ke kapu la, 'akāhi o luna nei.
'O Ka-lani 'o Kau-i-ke-ao-uli, 'alua o luna nei,
Pili lāua, ua mau paha.

Birth Chant (closing verse)

Born was Kū, let him remain above.
Who shall be below? Who indeed?

From Hāloa men came forth, chiefs multiplied.
Chief Ka-mehameha was conceived above,
    the first chief, the first up here.
The Chiefess Kau-i-ka-'alaneo was the second up here.
They joined, clung together. Was it not so?
Ka-lani-nui-kua-liholiho was the first
    to inherit the kapus, the first up here.
Chief Kau-i-ke-ao-uli was the second up here.
Brothers are they, close joined: they hold firm to
    one another.

From The Echo of Our Song *by Mary Kawena Pukui and Alfons L. Korn, The University Press of Hawaii, 1973*

Introduction

*K*amehameha III: Kauikeaouli is a biography of the Hawaiian kingdom's third ruler. A biography is a written story of a person's life and is based upon historical records. This story tells about the significant events of Kauikeaouli's life. It starts with his birth and childhood and continues through his reign of nearly thirty years.

From 1810 to 1893 the kingdom of Hawai'i was ruled by eight monarchs. Of all these rulers Kauikeaouli reigned the longest. Under his leadership Hawai'i changed from an isolated island kingdom to a recognized member of the modern world. Many of the things he did as king still influence life in Hawai'i today.

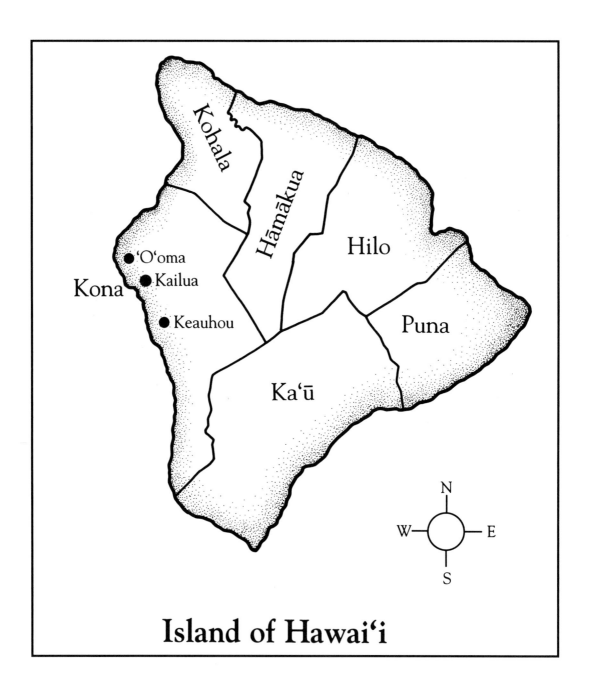

Island of Hawai‘i

Birth of a Prince

Kauikeaouli was born at Keauhou, Kona, on the island of Hawai'i. Many people believe that Kauikeaouli means "Placed in the Dark Clouds." Although the exact date of his birth is not known, some historians believe it was August 11, 1814. Kauikeaouli chose St. Patrick's Day, March 17, as his birth date after he learned about Saint Patrick from an Irish friend.

Kamehameha III's full name was Kauikeaouli Kaleiopapa Kuakamanolani Mahinalani Kalaninuiwaiakua Keaweawe'ulaokalani. His father was Kamehameha, Hawai'i's first monarch. His mother was Keōpūolani, one of the highest ranking *ali'i* in Hawai'i.

Kauikeaouli's older brother, 'Iolani Liholiho, was born in 1797. The youngest in the family was Princess Nāhi'ena'ena, who was born in 1815.

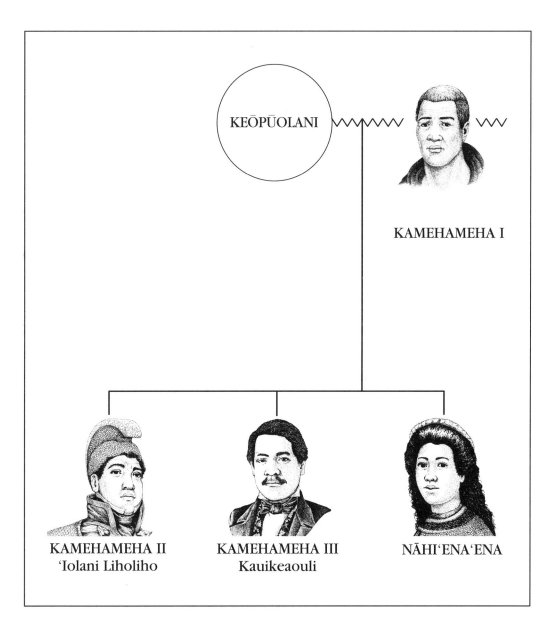

KEŌPŪOLANI

KAMEHAMEHA I

KAMEHAMEHA II
'Iolani Liholiho

KAMEHAMEHA III
Kauikeaouli

NĀHI'ENA'ENA

Kauikeaouli Genealogy

Early Childhood

It was the custom for an *ali'i*, or chief, to choose another *ali'i* to raise his child. It was believed that this helped strengthen the political and social bonds between the *ali'i* families. Keōpūolani chose Chief Kaikio'ewa to raise Kauikeaouli as his *hānai*, or adopted, son.

Chief Kaikio'ewa took Kauikeaouli to his home in 'O'oma, Kekaha, in North Kona. He taught the young prince the ways of his people. The little boy received much love and attention from the chief and his family.

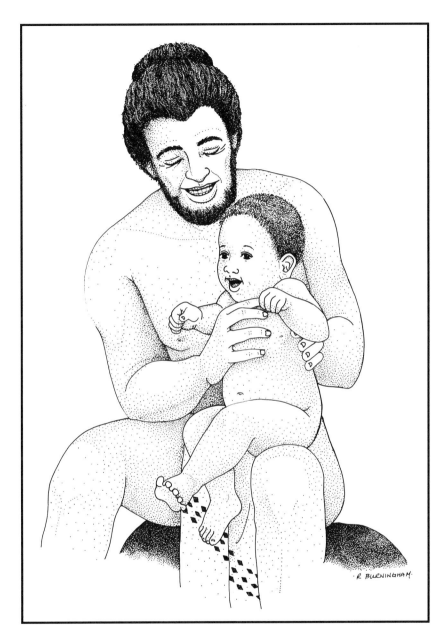

Chief Kaikioʻewa with his hānai *son Kauikeaouli*

Kauikeaouli enjoyed playing with toy boats built like the first foreign ships that came to Hawai‘i. Each had little brass cannons which could be loaded with gunpowder. Kauikeaouli was greatly amused by the firing of the cannons.

Kauikeaouli with his toy boat

Breaking of the Eating *Kapu*

When Kauikeaouli was about five years old, his mother sent for him to join her at Kailua, Kona. This happened shortly after his older brother Liholiho became king.

Young Kauikeaouli and Liholiho were present when Keōpūolani ate pork and a forbidden kind of banana. Under the *kapu* system, or traditional Hawaiian law, such foods were not allowed to women.

In addition men and women were not allowed to eat together. Within a few months Liholiho ate openly with his mother and other women. This act signaled the breaking of Hawai'i's *kapu* system.

Liholiho ate with the women, breaking the eating kapu

The Missionaries Arrive

In 1820 the first American Protestant missionaries arrived in Hawai'i, bringing with them the Christian religion. They taught Keōpūolani this new religion. She wanted Kauikeaouli to learn this new religion, too.

The young prince was one of the first children to be educated by the missionaries. They taught him the Christian religion and introduced him to the English language.

Kauikeaouli being taught the Christian religion

Liholiho's Successor

When Kamehameha I died in 1819 Kauikeaouli's older brother, Liholiho, took the name Kamehameha II.

Four years later, in 1823, he decided to visit England. Liholiho had long wanted to see the capital and meet the leaders of Great Britain.

Like his father, Kamehameha I, Liholiho wanted the Hawaiian kingdom to be under the protection of Great Britain. He was very curious to travel to that powerful country and learn more about it.

Liholiho, Kamehameha II

Before leaving Hawai'i, Liholiho and the council of chiefs made plans for governing the kingdom in his absence.

Kauikeaouli was chosen to succeed Liholiho should Liholiho die while away from Hawai'i. Because Kauikeaouli was still a child, only about ten years old, Liholiho and the high chiefs chose Ka'ahumanu, the *kuhina nui* or co-ruler, to serve as regent. A regent is a person chosen to rule for a monarch when he or she is absent or too young to rule.

Liholiho and Queen Kamāmalu sailed from Hawai'i on the English whaling ship *L'Aigle* in November 1823. They arrived in England in May 1824. Sadly, both the king and queen caught the measles and died in London in July 1824. On May 6, 1825, almost a year later, their bodies were returned to Honolulu on the English warship *Blonde*.

Liholiho, Kamāmalu and Liliha at the theatre, June 4th, 1824

from a drawing by J.W. Gear, as published in
Hawaii: A Pictorial History, *Bishop Museum Press, 1969*

The Boy King and Ka'ahumanu

uring a special ceremony in Honolulu on June 6, 1825, Kauikeaouli was proclaimed king of Hawai'i. To the people he said, "Where are you, chiefs, guardians, commoners? I greet you. Hear what I say! My kingdom I give to God. The righteous chief shall be my chief, the children of the commoners who do right shall be my people, my kingdom shall be one of letters."

Kauikeaouli, the "boy king," was only ten years old. His words pleased Ka'ahumanu who, as regent, was the actual ruler of the Hawaiian kingdom.

Kaʻahumanu, kuhina nui *of Hawaiʻi*

When Kauikeaouli was fifteen he took part in the dedication ceremony of the first Kawaiaha'o Church. At that time Kawaiaha'o Church was a large thatched house of worship. The young king wore a special blue uniform given him by a British captain. How handsome he looked!

Kauikeaouli attended council meetings as the king. At one of the meetings he was asked about making the "Ten Commandments" the new laws of the kingdom. Kauikeaouli was unsure and did not answer at first. Finally he said, "It would be best to wait." He did not know whether his people wanted Christian laws.

Young Kauikeaouli in a blue uniform given him by a British naval captain

In 1832 Ka'ahumanu died from an intestinal illness. She was about sixty-five years old. Ka'ahumanu had been a powerful ruler. With advice from the missionaries she had made new laws, encouraged education and helped Hawai'i become a largely Christian nation.

Ka'ahumanu ruled the kingdom for seven years

23

Kīnaʻu Becomes
Kuhina Nui

Kaʻahumanu had ruled the kingdom for seven years, from 1825 to 1832. During that time Kauikeaouli had been "the boy king." But at the age of eighteen he was anxious to become the real king. The high chiefs, however, did not feel he was responsible enough to rule alone.

The chiefs, therefore, chose Chiefess Kīnaʻu to be the new *kuhina nui* of Hawaiʻi. Kīnaʻu was a daughter of Kamehameha I and Kalākua. She was twenty-seven years of age and Kauikeaouli's half-sister.

Kīna'u, kuhina nui *of Hawai'i*

Kīna'u and Kauikeaouli did not always agree on what was best for the people. He wanted to buy a ship, for example, but she would not allow it. She knew that the government could not afford such an expense. Kauikeaouli resented having to share his power with Kīna'u and the high chiefs.

Kauikeaouli Rebels

In anger Kauikeaouli rebelled. He went against Kīna'u and the chiefs and on March 15, 1833, took control of the government. He terminated Kīna'u's position as *kuhina nui*. He told the people that he alone would rule. He canceled most of the strict laws and brought back many of the old customs. Once again people could dance the *hula* and play games like *'ulu maika* and *pūhenehene*. Gambling and drinking increased and many people stopped going to school and church.

Once again the people could dance the hula

During 1833 and 1834 there was confusion and uncertainty. Kauikeaouli wavered between ruling alone and giving in to pressure from the older chiefs. He saw the anger in Kīna'u. He knew the missionaries were upset. It was clear that the powerful few did not support his actions.

Kauikeaouli realized that he could not be as strong a ruler as his father. Bending to outside pressures, in 1835 he was forced to return to sharing his powers with Kīna'u and the Council of Chiefs. Kīna'u returned as *kuhina nui,* to serve as co-ruler, and Kauikeaouli placed most of the responsibilities in her hands. Things settled back to the way they had been before Kauikeaouli's actions of 1833. People gradually returned to school and began attending church again.

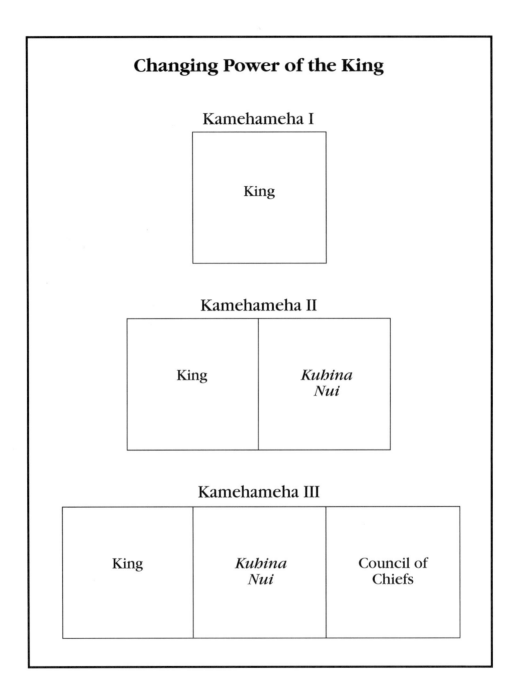

Changing Power of the King

Kamehameha I

King

Kamehameha II

King	*Kuhina Nui*

Kamehameha III

King	*Kuhina Nui*	Council of Chiefs

Kauikeaouli was forced to return to sharing his powers

Kauikeaouli and Nāhiʻenaʻena

During his childhood Kauikeaouli experienced much sadness. By the time he was ten years old Kauikeaouli had lost his father, mother and older brother. He and his younger sister Nāhiʻenaʻena were raised by other *aliʻi*. Missionaries continued to be their teachers.

In July of 1834 something happened which deeply troubled the missionaries. Kauikeaouli married Nāhiʻenaʻena. He was twenty years old and she was nineteen. Marriages between family members were an old custom among *aliʻi*. They believed such marriages helped to increase their *mana*, or spiritual power.

"Kamehameha III as a boy,"
by Robert Dampier (1825)

Portrait courtesy of the Honolulu Academy of Arts

"Nahienaena, sister of Kamehameha III,"
by Robert Dampier (1825)
Portrait courtesy of the Honolulu Academy of Arts

Marriages between close family members were not allowed by the Christian faith. For this reason the missionaries and Christian chiefs would not accept the marriage. After much pressure Kauikeaouli and Nāhiʻenaʻena ended their marriage of seven months. The young king's hope of ruling Hawaiʻi with his sister was not to be.

Tragically Nāhiʻenaʻena died from an illness two years later in December 1836. She was only twenty-one years old. With his entire immediate family gone a sorrowful Kauikeaouli felt very much alone.

The king's sister and their mother, Keōpūolani, are buried in the cemetery of Waiola Church in Lahaina, Maui.

Tombstone of Keōpūolani and Nāhiʻenaʻena in the cemetery of Waiola Church, Lahaina, Maui

Kauikeaouli Marries Kalama

Following the advice of his high chiefs, Kauikeaouli married Chiefess Kalama in a Christian ceremony in 1837. Kalama was the *hānai* daughter of Miriam Kekāuluohi and Charles Kanaʻina, parents of William Lunalilo.

For the next eight years the king and queen lived in Lahaina, the capital of the kingdom. They had two children but each died soon after birth.

Queen Kalama, wife of Kamehameha III

Hānai Son,
Alexander Liholiho

In 1834 Kīna'u, Kauikeaouli's half-sister, had given birth to a son, Alexander Liholiho. Kauikeaouli took Alexander as his *hānai* child. He raised his young nephew as his own son, preparing him to be the next monarch of Hawai'i, Kamehameha IV.

First row: Queen Kalama, Kamehameha III, Victoria Kamāmalu;
second row: Alexander Liholiho and Lot Kapuāiwa

Photo courtesy of Bishop Museum

Kekāuluohi Becomes *Kuhina Nui*

Kīnaʻu died in 1839. Like Kaʻahumanu, she had continued the policy of strictly enforcing laws inspired by missionary teachings. Her sister, Miriam Kekāuluohi, now became the *kuhina nui* of Hawaiʻi.

Miriam Kekāuluohi, kuhina nui
Photo courtesy of Bishop Museum

Religious Freedom

In 1827 Catholic missionaries from France came to the islands to establish their religion. They were not welcomed by the Protestant missionaries and some Hawaiian leaders. Rivalries arose between the Hawaiian members of these two religious groups.

Kamehameha III tired of the continued conflicts. In 1839 he ordered that the persecution, or harassment, of Catholics be stopped. Later the Constitution of 1840 stated that "...there should be complete freedom in the matter of religion."

Despite this law, opposition between Catholics and Protestants continued. In 1843 Kauikeaouli issued a proclamation to the people directing them to avoid conflict and live in peace.

In 1842, after five years of construction, the Protestants' "Stone Church" at Kawaiaha'o was completed and dedicated. Kauikeaouli attended this church but never became a member.

Kawaiaha'o Church, completed in 1842

"A Kingdom of Learning"

"Chiefs and people, give ear to my remarks! My kingdom shall be a kingdom of learning." These words, spoken by Kauikeaouli, showed he believed that education was very important. He believed education would prepare his people for the changes taking place in Hawai'i.

American Protestant missionaries also believed in education. Through education they spread their religious teachings among the people.

With the encouragement of Kauikeaouli, missionary teachers started many schools. They taught students, most of whom were adults, to read and write in Hawaiian.

Portions of the Bible were translated and printed in Hawaiian. These Bible translations were used as the primary textbooks. One result of this instruction was that thousands of Hawaiians became members of (predominantly Protestant) western churches.

The first schools were simple grass houses with mats on the floor. There were no chairs or tables. Later Kauikeaouli established permanent buildings built of coral blocks, lava rocks or adobe bricks.

Lahainaluna School

By 1830 schools were established on every island. However there were not enough missionaries to teach the growing number of Hawaiians wanting to become students. To meet the need for more teachers, Lahainaluna School opened on Maui in 1831 to train Hawaiian men for teaching. Lahainaluna became the most important school in Hawai'i during the reign of Kamehameha III. Many of its graduates became important citizens of the kingdom. It is still operating, now as a public boarding school, in Lahaina.

R BURNINGHAM

Lahainaluna School opened in Lahaina, Maui, in 1831

The Chiefs' Children's School

In 1839 Kauikeaouli opened the Chiefs' Children's School in Honolulu. He felt that future rulers must be prepared to rule a kingdom which now included both Hawaiians and foreigners. The Chiefs' Children's School was a very special school. In 1846 its name was changed to the Royal School.

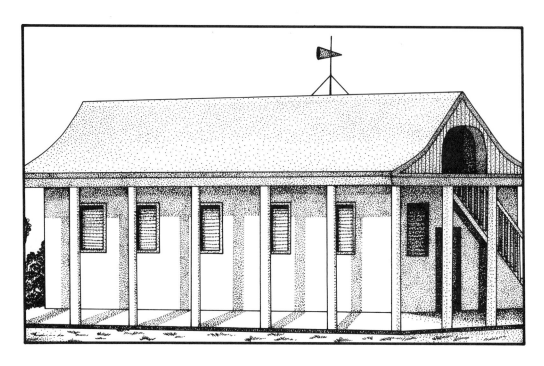

The Royal School

Only sixteen Hawaiian children of the highest chiefly rank attended the Royal School. Five of them later became rulers of the kingdom. They were Alexander Liholiho, who became Kamehameha IV; Lot Kapuāiwa, who became Kamehameha V; William Lunalilo; David Kalākaua and Lydia Liliʻuokalani. Princess Bernice Pauahi Bishop also attended the Royal School. When he was about to die, Lot Kapuāiwa asked Pauahi to succeed him as ruler. She declined the throne and later founded the Kamehameha Schools.

Public Education

Recognizing the growing importance of education, the government took over direction and support of the schools. The Constitution of 1840 provided for free public education and required all children to attend school. Gradually the training of teachers improved, more textbooks were provided, better schools were built and more money was spent to run the schools.

Hilo Boys' Boarding School in 1840

By 1850 English was the language used in business, government and foreign relations. Many Hawaiians wanted to have their children learn English, hoping this would prepare them for a better future. A few English language schools were started to support this goal.

Toward the end of Kauikeaouli's reign there were 423 schools in Hawai'i with an enrollment of over twelve thousand students. Most of the schools were elementary schools using Hawaiian as the language of instruction. This greatly pleased Kamehameha III. His kingdom had indeed become a "kingdom of learning."

Foreigners Demand Changes

When Kauikeaouli was a younger man people talked about his cheerful-looking face and gentle manner. By the time he was thirty years of age he looked much older. His physical appearance seemed to reflect the pressure he faced governing a Hawai'i troubled by the new mix of Hawaiian and western values.

Kauikeaouli at thirty

Kauikeaouli loved his people and tried his best to fulfill their needs through the old customs and traditions. But foreigners, not used to the way things were done in Hawai'i, wanted changes. Many of them did not understand or respect the Hawaiian ways. They raised questions and caused problems. Captains from visiting ships forced unfair demands upon the king. This was a troublesome period!

Kauikeaouli had never traveled to the foreigners' countries and was not comfortable with their many foreign languages. He did not fully understand their foreign laws and customs.

The king decided to seek advice from a few foreigners whom he trusted. He spent much time with them. They discussed changes that would meet the demands of the foreigners and still be best for his Hawaiian people.

How much change would be needed before Hawaiians and foreigners could live together in peace? This was the great challenge for Kamehameha III.

Kauikeaouli met with foreigners he trusted

A Constitutional Government

The Declaration of Rights—1839

One of the first changes made by Kamehameha III took place in government. Kamehameha III was convinced that all people should have certain rights. In 1839 he put these rights in writing in a document called The Declaration of Rights.

> "God hath made of one blood all nations of men, to dwell on the face of the earth in unity and blessedness. God has also bestowed certain rights alike on all men, and all chiefs, and all people of all lands.

> "These are some of the rights which he has given alike to every man and every chief, life, limb, liberty, the labor of his hands, and productions of his mind...."

The Constitution of 1840

The next year an even more important event happened. Kamehameha III granted his people laws which, for the first time, explained in writing how the government would be run. These special laws became the Constitution of 1840, the first written constitution ever granted to the people of Hawai'i.

A constitution is a document in which the basic laws and principles of a government are written down. The Constitution of 1840 defined the powers and duties of government officials who were charged with keeping its laws. The Declaration of Rights was made the preamble, or introduction, to this constitution.

By signing the constitution Kamehameha III agreed to not only share more of his powers, but also to limit them. For the first time Hawaiian men from the *maka'āinana* (working class) would take part in government. Foreigners who became citizens of the kingdom could also participate.

The Constitution of 1840 granted the *maka'āinana* the right to vote, be elected or appointed to office, and help make the laws of the kingdom. Hawai'i would be governed by the king along with the *kuhina nui,* the chiefs and the *maka'āinana*.

Changing Government under Kamehameha III

1825

Regency

1835

King	*Kuhina Nui*	Council of Chiefs

1840

Constitutional Government			
King	*Kuhina Nui*	Council of Chiefs	*Maka'āinana*

Takeover of the Kingdom

In 1843, three years after the signing of the constitution, the kingdom suffered a serious blow. With his ship's cannons pointing at Honolulu, British Captain Lord George Paulet seized control of the Hawaiian kingdom. He claimed this action was necessary to protect the rights of British residents in the islands. On February 25, 1843, the Hawaiian flag was lowered and the British flag hoisted in its place.

The Hawaiian flag was lowered on February 25, 1843

Hawai'i had never before been ruled by a foreign power. Kamehameha III was furious! He saw the fear, anger and confusion among his people. However, to avoid any loss of life, he had to give in to Paulet. Kauikeaouli assured his people that the kingdom would be restored once the British government learned about the forceful takeover.

Restoration of the Kingdom

Five months later, on July 31, 1843, the king's hope for the return of the Hawaiian monarchy came true. With the help of British Admiral Richard Thomas, the Hawaiian flag was once again raised over the islands. The kingdom was restored!

A colorful ceremony was held in an area near the intersection of Ward Avenue and Beretania Street in Honolulu. Today this place is a park whose name honors Admiral Thomas—Thomas Square.

British Admiral Richard Thomas

In a thanksgiving service at Kawaiahaʻo Church, Kamehameha III spoke the words that became the motto of the state of Hawaiʻi: *"Ua mau ke ea o ka ʻāina i ka pono."* This has most commonly been translated as: "The life of the land is perpetuated in righteousness."

The celebration continued for ten days. For years following that first celebration, Kauikeaouli made Restoration Day, July 31, the most important holiday of the year.

UA MAU KE EA O KA AINA I KA PONO

Hawai'i's coat of arms

An Independent Nation

$\mathcal{K}$auikeaouli tried to meet the needs of both Hawaiians and foreigners living in the kingdom. But, at the same time, he was also faced with pressures from outside the kingdom. Many foreign countries, for instance, continued to make unfair demands.

Unequal Treaties

Most of the foreigners living in Hawai'i were from the United States, Great Britain and France. Their governments felt responsible for their protection. To ensure the rights of the foreigners, written agreements, or treaties, were made by their governments with the Hawaiian government.

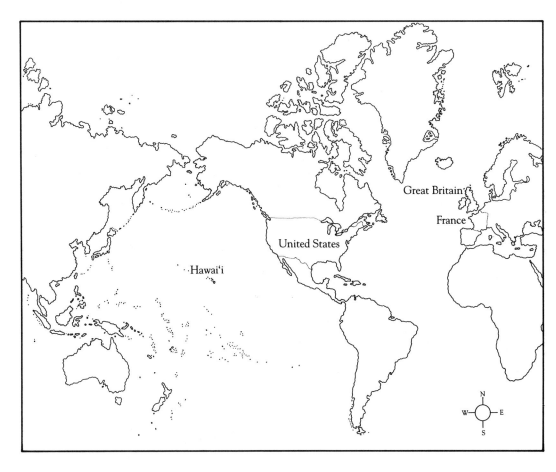

Foreigners living in Hawai'i were largely from the United States, Great Britain and France

In theory treaties should be agreeable to both countries. However weaker nations are sometimes forced to accept the terms of treaties proposed by stronger nations—whether they agree or not. This was the case with the Hawaiian kingdom. Many "unequal treaties" were forced upon Kamehameha III and his government.

Recognition of Independence

Kauikeaouli wanted his kingdom to have a more secure and respected place in the world. He wrote letters to the president of the United States, the queen of Great Britain and the king of France. Kamehameha III wanted the leaders of these countries to recognize the independence of the Hawaiian kingdom.

The letters were to be delivered in person to an official of each nation. Three representatives from the king's government were chosen to undertake this mission. They left the islands in 1842.

Upon their arrival in each country they presented the letters to officials of the country. They then held discussions on the need for formal recognition of the Hawaiian kingdom. They also asked for treaties equally favorable to each of the nations involved.

In 1844 agreements were reached. The United States, Great Britain and France recognized the Hawaiian kingdom as an independent nation. Hawai'i was a member of the "family of nations." From then on treaties with other countries could be developed on a more equal basis.

From Lahaina to Honolulu

During the 1830s and 1840s Honolulu was developing into an important city. This was largely due to its harbor. Captains of foreign ships liked the relative calm of Honolulu Harbor, offering shelter from the usual trade winds. As shipping traffic and business activities increased so too did the population.

Because of Honolulu's growing importance Kamehameha III moved his capital from Lahaina, Maui, to Honolulu in 1845. His new home was a fine house built in 1844 by Kekūanao'a, governor of O'ahu. It became known as Hale Ali'i, or "House of the Chief."

Hawai'i's first royal palace, Hale Ali'i, built on the site of the present 'Iolani Palace; named 'Iolani in 1863 by Kamehameha V for his brother Alexander Liholiho 'Iolani, Kamehameha IV

R. BURNINGHAM

Land Ownership

The Right to Own Land

The right to own land in Hawai'i was the major demand made by foreigners. They wanted to buy land but land in Hawai'i had never been sold. These foreigners did not understand the Hawaiian attitude towards land. In their western cultures owning the land one lived on was a right. They felt that they should have this right in Hawai'i too.

Many foreigners wanted to start businesses in the islands. Some had already done so. How could they be sure their investments would be safe if they did not own the land? Some foreigners needed large areas of land in order to grow plantation crops such as sugar cane. This would not be possible, they thought, without owning the land.

Then there were those foreigners who believed that owning one's land would benefit native Hawaiians as well. Their western way of thinking led them to believe that if Hawaiians owned their own land they could improve their standard of living and become more productive citizens.

Demands by foreigners for land increased.
Kauikeaouli felt the pressure. In 1841 the king
offered the foreigners long-term leases of land. A
lease is a contract by which a person rents land for a
certain period of time. The king hoped that this offer
would satisfy the foreigners. But this was not what
the foreigners wanted. They looked upon this offer
as an attempt to deprive them of their rights.

Kauikeaouli explained, "We lay no claims whatever
to any property of theirs, either growing or erected
on the soil. That is theirs, exclusively. We simply
claim the soil itself...."

The Hawaiian Belief

The idea of owning the *'āina* (land) was hard for Hawaiians to grasp. In Hawaiian culture no individual owned land—it belonged to the *akua* (gods). The *mō'ī* (king) and his *ali'i nui* (high chiefs) controlled the land while the *konohiki* (lesser chiefs) managed it. The *maka'āinana* lived on the land. In return they gave the *ali'i nui* their service and a portion of what they produced.

In the Hawaiian culture land was owned by the gods and cared for by the people

The chiefs did not want changes made in the Hawaiian land system. Some felt that they would lose control over the land, the people who lived there and the products made by them.

The chiefs also feared that foreigners would gradually gain control of the kingdom. What would happen to the *maka'ainana?* How could Kamehameha III safeguard the rights and welfare of his own people?

The Land Commission

Although Kauikeaouli and his chiefs tried to keep Hawaiian land from being sold to foreigners, it was not to be. Foreigners continued to complain and demand changes.

In 1845, acting upon the advice of a few trusted foreigners, the king created a "Land Commission." The Land Commission was a five-member committee appointed to study the land claims of both Hawaiians and foreigners. Their decisions would be final.

What happened during the next five years would change the land system in Hawai'i forever.

The Māhele

On January 27, 1848, the Māhele, or division of lands, began. With the Māhele the foreign concept of "land ownership" was established in Hawai'i. The traditional relationship Hawaiians had held with their *'āina* would never be the same.

The Land Commission had determined that the land should be divided into equal thirds. One third would go to the *ali'i*, one third would go to the government and the final third would go to the *maka'āinana*.

Kamehameha III was given the responsibility for sharing the lands between the chiefs and himself. The king divided up land between himself and 245 chiefs. His lands were called "Crown Lands." Those for the chiefs were called *"Konohiki* Lands." This division was recorded in the *Māhele Book.*

The Māhele Book

Photo courtesy of Bishop Museum

Six weeks later, on March 7, 1848, Kauikeaouli gave a large portion of his Crown Lands to "the chiefs and people of my Kingdom." This portion was then called "Government Lands" and was also recorded in the *Māhele Book*. Of the total lands available 23 percent were "Crown Lands," 37 percent were "Government Lands" and 40 percent were "*Konohiki* Lands."

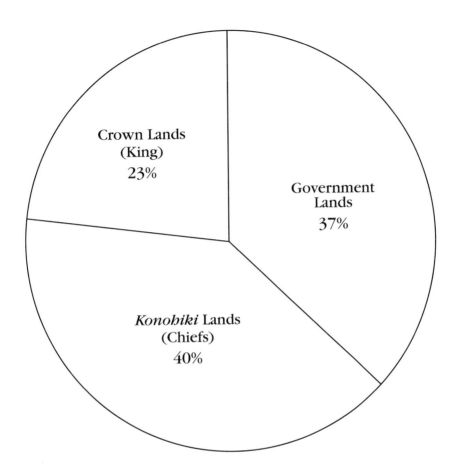

The division of lands on March 7, 1848

After the king divided his Crown Lands that March day the Māhele was officially over. It had lasted a total of forty-one days. From that time until today, the *Māhele Book* and the land awards granted by the Land Commission have been the basis for all land titles, or ownership documents, in Hawai'i.

The Resident Alien Act of 1850

It did not take long for the aliens, or foreigners, to get what they wanted. The Resident Alien Act of July 10, 1850, gave them the right to buy land in fee simple. Fee simple means that land is owned rather than leased. It also means that individuals who own land may sell that land or pass it on to their heirs. This is the system the foreigners understood and wanted for Hawai'i.

The Kuleana Act of 1850

As for the *maka'āinana,* the Kuleana Act of
August 1850 made it possible for them to own
land in fee simple. *Kuleana* is the Hawaiian word
for responsibility. Therefore *kuleana* also became
the term for land that people had lived on
and cultivated.

The *maka'āinana* had to follow certain steps
before they could own their land. First, they had to
have their *kuleana* surveyed, or measured for size
and boundaries. Then they had to present their
claims to the Land Commission, showing that they
had a right to those *kuleana.* They also needed to
file their claim by 1854.

Unfortunately many *maka'āinana* did not do what the law required. They lacked the knowledge, experience and money to pay for surveys. In addition many missed the 1854 filing deadline. Only 13,514 claims were filed and the number of *kuleana* grants actually awarded was just 9,337. *Maka'āinana* ended up with less than 1 percent of the total land available.

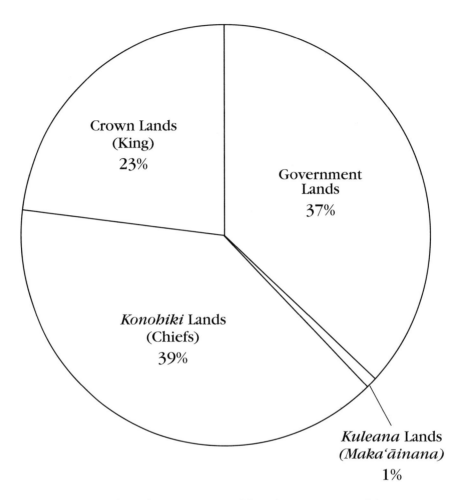

Crown Lands
(King)
23%

Government
Lands
37%

Konohiki Lands
(Chiefs)
39%

Kuleana Lands
(*Maka'āinana)*
1%

In 1854 the maka'āinana *owned less than 1 percent of the
total lands available*

Most Hawaiians did not own any land. Some of those who did own their *kuleana* lost it later because they did not pay land taxes.

Then there were those who lost their land because they did not occupy, or live on, their *kuleana*. This was due to the "adverse possession" law. Under this law a person was allowed to claim land that had not been occupied by its owner for ten years or more.

As many Hawaiians lost their *kuleana* for one reason or another, foreigners were ready to buy and sell those *kuleana*.

The Constitution of 1852

By 1852 Kamehameha III realized that the Constitution of 1840 was out of date. The responsibilities of the government had greatly increased so a new constitution was written to meet those responsibilities.

The Constitution of 1852 was more liberal, or generous, than the Constitution of 1840. It gave greater power to the people in running the government.

By his actions, Kamehameha III gave up much of the monarch's power. Never again would a Hawaiian ruler have the power his father, Kamehameha I, once had. The Constitutions of 1840 and 1852 changed the structure of Hawaiian government forever.

Threats to Hawai'i's Peace and Security

In 1844 the United States, Great Britain and France had recognized the Hawaiian kingdom as an independent nation. Unfortunately, this recognition did not bring the peace and security Kamehameha III had hoped for. Several events at this time caused the king and his people to feel uneasy and uncertain about the future.

Expansion by the United States

By the 1840s the United States had reached the shores of the Pacific Ocean. It expanded its territory by acquiring California and Oregon. Would Hawai'i be next?

Gold in California

Then, in 1848, gold was discovered in California. People rushed to California to try to make their fortune. From 1849 to 1854 many of them came to Hawai'i to spend the winter season. With them came rumors and reports about overthrowing the Hawaiian monarchy and setting up a new government.

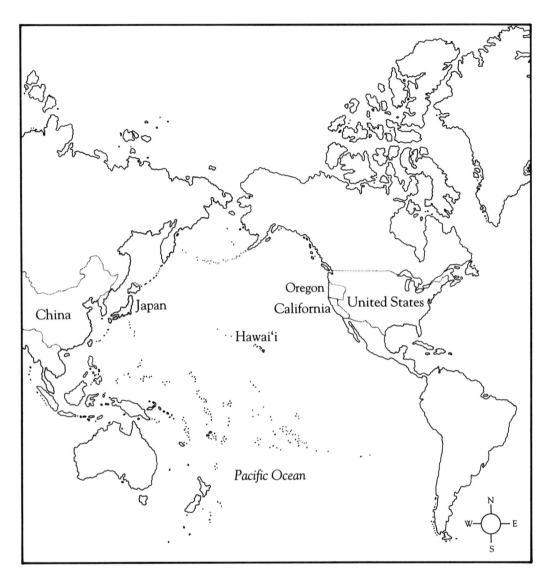

The United States acquired California and Oregon. Would Hawai'i be next?
Hawai'i's strategic location was an ideal stopover.

A Strategic Location

Meanwhile foreigners focused on Hawai'i's strategic location in the Pacific. The islands were an ideal stopover for traders traveling to China and Japan. The United States recognized the importance of Pearl Harbor. As early as 1845 it thought about acquiring the harbor to serve as both a naval and commercial port.

Declining Hawaiian Population

Adding to Kauikeaouli's worries was the declining health and population of his people. When Captain Cook arrived in the islands, in 1778, there were about three hundred thousand Hawaiians. In 1825, the year Kauikeaouli became king, there were only half as many, or about one hundred fifty thousand Hawaiians. Tens of thousands had died from diseases brought by foreigners.

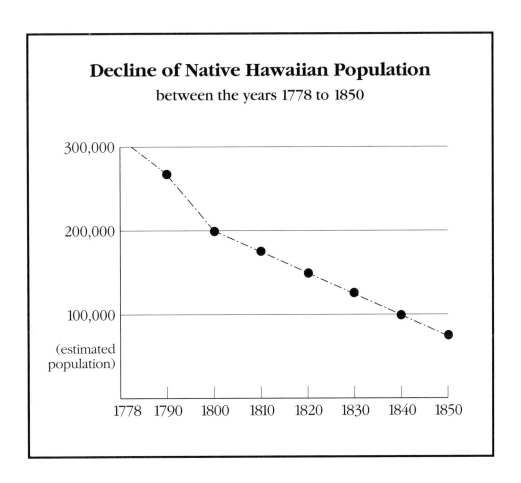

Decline of Native Hawaiian Population
between the years 1778 to 1850

300,000

200,000

100,000

(estimated population)

1778 1790 1800 1810 1820 1830 1840 1850

To make matters worse, a smallpox epidemic broke out on Oʻahu in 1853. Smallpox is a highly contagious disease. Kamehameha III was alarmed at how fast his people were dying! Even though he tried to quarantine, or separate, the sick from the healthy, twenty-five hundred Hawaiians died in the epidemic. By 1854 there were only seventy thousand Hawaiians left in the kingdom. Meanwhile the foreign population in Hawaiʻi continued to grow.

The smallpox hospital at Waikīkī, about 1853

Troubles with the French

Troubles with the French increased with the coming of the new French consul in 1848. He accused the Hawaiian government of mistreatment and discrimination against the twelve French citizens living in Hawai'i.

In 1849 two French warships arrived in Honolulu Harbor. The French admiral sent a list of ten demands to the king, who rejected them. One demand was to give the French Catholics as much control of the public education system as the Protestants.

In anger, the French forces came ashore, wrecked the fort by the harbor and vandalized the governor's house. They stole the king's yacht, called the *Kamehameha III*. The yacht was never returned.

The Question of Annexation

It is not surprising then that, toward the end of his reign, Kamehameha III thought about annexing, or joining, his kingdom with the United States. He wanted to do what was best for his people. He believed that the United States would protect and care for his people.

Annexation, however, would not occur during Kauikeaouli's rule. Hawai'i would remain an independent kingdom for the next thirty-nine years.

Death of Kamehameha III

King Kamehameha III, Kauikeaouli Kaleiopapa Kuakamanolani Mahinalani Kalaninuiwaiakua Keaweaweʻulaokalani, died on December 16, 1854. He had been in poor health for more than a year. Kauikeaouli was only forty years old.

The Hawaiian people were deeply saddened. They felt a great loss as their beloved king was laid to rest in the royal burial place on the grounds of ʻIolani Palace. Eleven years later, in 1865, his remains, along with those of other *aliʻi,* were taken to the royal burial site at Mauna ʻAla in Nuʻuanu.

Kauikeaouli's funeral procession (attributed to Mesnard, ca. 1870)

Photo courtesy of Bishop Museum

The Kamehameha tombstone at Mauna ʻAla in Nuʻuanu

The Kingdom Survives!

Kamehameha III reigned for nearly thirty years. He was continually challenged by growing foreign pressures. He met those challenges by making significant changes affecting the lives of the people of Hawai'i.

The kingdom was now governed under a constitution. Free public education and religious freedom were firmly established.

The Māhele made it possible for people to own land. Rightly or wrongly, Kamehameha III allowed the Māhele to take place because he believed it could benefit his kingdom.

Today Kauikeaouli is remembered as a ruler who, first and foremost, worked diligently to ensure the survival of the Hawaiian kingdom. With his quiet manner and wise judgment he met each challenge with the love and support of his people.

Kauikeaouli, Kamehameha III, about 1850, artist unknown
Portrait in the collection of Kamehameha Schools Bernice Pauahi Bishop Estate

114

Bibliography

Apple, Russ. "A King's Secret Rendezvous" from "Tales of Old Hawaii." *Honolulu Star-Bulletin* 31 January 1985.

Bailey, Paul. *Those Kings and Queens of Old Hawaii, A Mele to Their Memory.* Los Angeles: Westernlore Books, 1975.

Curtis, Caroline. *Builders of Hawaii.* Honolulu: The Kamehameha Schools Press, 1966.

Daws, Gavan. *Shoal of Time: A History of the Hawaiian Islands.* New York: Macmillan Company, 1968; Honolulu: The University of Hawaii Press, 1974.

Day, A. Grove. *A Biographical Dictionary, History Makers of Hawaii.* Honolulu: Mutual Publishing of Honolulu, 1984.

"Elaborate Funeral of Kamehameha III Described in Fine Detail by Witness." *Honolulu Star-Bulletin* 4 July 1931, p. 6.

Feher, Joseph. *Hawaii: A Pictorial History*. Honolulu: Bishop Museum, 1969.

Gwenfread, Allen. *Hawaii's Iolani Palace and Its Kings and Queens*. Honolulu: Aloha Graphics and Sales, 1978.

Harrison, Samuel. *The White King*. Garden City, N.Y.: Doubleday, 1950.

Holt, John Dominis. *Monarchy in Hawaii*. Honolulu: Topgallant Publishing Co., Ltd., 1971.

Jarves, James Jackson. *History of the Hawaiian Islands*. Honolulu: Henry M. Whitney, 1872.

Jarves, James Jackson. *Scenes and Scenery in the Sandwich Islands*. Boston: James Munroe & Co., 1843.

Judd, Bernice. *Voyages to Hawaii Before 1860*. Honolulu: Hawaiian Mission Children's Society, 1929.

Kamakau, Samuel M. *Ruling Chiefs of Hawaii*. Honolulu: The Kamehameha Schools Press, 1961 and 1992.

Kameʻeleihiwa, Lilikala. *Native Land and Foreign Desires*. Honolulu: Bishop Museum Press, 1992.

"King Tried to Sell His Crown." *The Pacific Commercial Advertiser* 18 January 1903, Vol. XXXVII, No. 6375.

Kuykendall, Ralph S. *The Hawaiian Kingdom, Vol. I, 1778-1854, Foundation and Transformation*. Honolulu: The University Press of Hawaii, 1980.

"Letters from the People—A Munificent Monarch."
The Honolulu Advertiser 27 July 1937, p. 18.

Mellen, Kathleen Dickinson. *The Gods Depart, A Saga
of the Hawaiian Kingdom, 1832-1873.* New York:
Hastings House, Publishers, 1956.

"Memory of Kamehameha III Ever Will Be Dear";
"Unveiling of Bronze Tablet to Mark Centenary";
"Review of Life and Efforts of Beloved Monarch of
Hawaii"; "Tuesday, Natal Day, Will Be Observed
by Daughters of Hawaii." *Honolulu Star-Bulletin*
14 March 1914, p. 9.

Menton, Linda and Tamura, Eileen. *A History of
Hawai'i.* Honolulu: Curriculum Research and
Development Group, College of Education,
University of Hawaii, 1989.

"Mystery Shrouds Birth Date of Kamehameha III But King Claimed March 17." *The Honolulu Advertiser* 17 March 1926, p. 9.

"Palace Ruins Change Hands." *The Sunday Star-Bulletin & Advertiser* 15 May 1988.

Richards, Mary A. *The Hawaiian Chiefs' Children's School, 1839-1850*. Rutland: Charles E. Tuttle Co., 1970.

Richards, William. *Memoirs of Keopuolani, Late Queen of the Sandwich Islands*. Boston: Crocker & Brewster, 1825.

Sinclair, Marjorie. *Nahienaena, Sacred Daughter of Hawaii*. Honolulu: The University Press of Hawaii, 1976.

Thrum, Thos. G. *Hawaiian Almanac & Annual for 1904*. Honolulu: Thos. G. Thrum, 1903.

Thrum, Thos. G. *Hawaiian Almanac and Annual for 1924*. Honolulu: Thos. G. Thrum, 1923, p. 126.

Wisniewski, Richard A. *The Rise and Fall of the Hawaiian Kingdom*. Honolulu: Pacific Basin Enterprises, 1979.

Withington, Antoinette. *The Golden Cloak*. Honolulu: Hawaiian Press Book, 1953.

Wong, Helen and Carey, Robert K. *Hawaii's Royal History*. Honolulu: Hogarth Press, Hawaii, Inc., 1980.

"Young Royalty of Hawaii Nearly Century Ago Appear in Journal." *Honolulu Star-Bulletin* 15 March 1930.